POETRY MATTERS

Writing a Poem from the Inside Out

Other books about writing by
RALPH FLETCHER

A Writer's Notebook:
Unlocking the Writer Within You

Live Writing:
Breathing Life into Your Words

How Writers Work:
Finding a Process That Works for You

POETRY
MATTERS

Writing a Poem from the Inside Out

Ralph Fletcher

HarperTrophy®
An Imprint of HarperCollinsPublishers

HarperTrophy® is a registered trademark of
HarperCollins Publishers Inc.

Poetry Matters: Writing a Poem from the Inside Out
Copyright © 2002 by Ralph Fletcher
All rights reserved. No part of this book may be used or reproduced in any manner whatsoever without written permission except in the case of brief quotations embodied in critical articles and reviews. Printed in the United States of America. For information address HarperCollins Children's Books, a division of HarperCollins Publishers, 195 Broadway, New York, NY, 10007.

Library of Congress Cataloging-in-Publication Data
Fletcher, Ralph J.
Poetry matters : writing a poem from the inside out / Ralph Fletcher.
p. cm.
Includes bibliographical references.
ISBN 0-06-623599-5 (lib. bdg.) — ISBN 0-380-79703-8 (pbk.)
1. Poetry—Authorship—Juvenile literature. [1. Poetry. 2. Poetry—Authorship.
3. Creative writing.] I. Title.
PN1059.A9 F58 2002   2001024640
808.1—dc21   CIP
                                                                              AC

First HarperTrophy edition, 2002
Visit us on the World Wide Web!
www.harperchildrens.com

18 19 20 BRR 30 29 28 27 26

for Georgia Heard,
wise teacher and friend

Acknowledgments

In writing this book, I was assisted by the efforts of many people, including Ruth Katcher (my editor), Marian Reiner (my agent), Bev Gallagher, Aimee Buckner, and Ann Marie Corgill.

Andrea Luna helped me to shape my ideas on teaching poetry. J. Patrick Lewis, Janet S. Wong, and Kristine O'Connell George were very generous with their busy time. Thanks to the staff at Arrowpoint 17.

I am grateful to all the students whose poems—imaginative, playful, passionate—enriched this book.

Thanks always to JoAnn.

CONTENTS

PART ONE

Lighting the Spark

The Power of Poetry

One year I came home from college to spend Christmas with my family, and I was flat broke. I had gotten used to being a poor college student, but this year I didn't want to be broke for Christmas. I was tired of buying junky gifts for my parents, brothers, and sisters. This year I wanted to have enough money to buy nice presents.

I got a job washing dishes at a local seafood restaurant, stacking trays of dirty dishes and hauling away the clean dishes when they emerged from the dish-washing machine. It was hot, sweaty work, but on Christmas Eve the manager handed me five crisp twenty-dollar bills. I hurried out to do my shopping.

There was a shopping center close to my house. I was walking across the parking lot when I was startled to see my grandfather. He was leaning over a container of trash, picking through it.

"Grandpa?" I said. When I took a step closer I could see that even though the man was tall, thin, and bald he wasn't my grandfather. This ragged man had a ripped coat; he looked cold. All I could imagine was my grandfather pawing through trash, looking for something to eat on Christmas Eve. I walked up to him and pressed the five twenty-dollar bills into his cold hand.

"Merry Christmas," I mumbled.

"Th-thank you, son," the man stammered, looking at the money.

I wanted to tell him to use the money to buy a new coat, but somehow the words wouldn't come out. I turned around and started walking home.

"Merry Christmas!" the man yelled.

"Merry Christmas," I said, waving. When I walked away I felt good. But the good feeling lasted about one minute. My wallet was empty now. I didn't have any money to buy presents for my family.

It seemed pointless to go shopping after that, so I walked home. On the way I got the seed of an idea. I went straight to my room, took out some paper, and started to write. My brainstorm was to write a poem for each member of my family.

I started with one of my little sisters. She liked horses, so I wrote her a poem about a horse galloping on the beach. It took me about a half hour to write the poem, and when it was finished I decided it wasn't bad at all.

One of my brothers wanted to be an astronaut, so I wrote him a poem about outer space. After a while Mom called me down to join everyone in hanging stockings from the mantel. When we were finished I went back upstairs to work.

By ten o'clock I had done four poems, but I had eight brothers and sisters. My eyes started getting tired. It was hard work—talk about writing under deadline!—but it was fun trying to think of what each person would want his or her poem to be about. I wrote and wrote. By eleven my eyes were blurry but the poems were done.

I went down to the basement. Someone had given Dad a box of old paper, and I knew he wouldn't mind if I took some sheets. I copied each poem onto a piece of paper, trying to keep the letters neat and not make any spelling mistakes. When I finished copying a poem, I rolled up the paper and tied a red ribbon around the middle. It was almost 1 A.M. when I went downstairs and tucked each scrolled poem in a stocking hanging from the fireplace. Finally I could drag myself upstairs and go to bed.

Early the next morning I felt someone tugging the collar of my pajamas. When I wrenched open my eyes, I saw my three-year-old sister Carolyn standing by my bed. She was holding her Christmas stocking, all lumpy with presents, and I could see the scrolled poem sticking out the top.

"Listen!" she said in an excited voice. Gently she scrunched her stocking until I could hear the paper crinkling.

"There's something magic in there," she said, nodding her little head and looking straight at me. "There's *poetry* in there. Poetry!"

Maybe you've heard before that poetry is magic, and it made you roll your eyes, but I believe it's true. Poetry matters. At the most important moments, when everyone else is silent, poetry rises to speak.

A beloved teacher retires. Her students write a poem and, later, at the ceremony, read it aloud to honor her.

A big sister gets married. Her little sister writes a poem and reads it at the reception.

At funerals, graduations, fiftieth wedding anniversaries, birthday parties, at the inauguration of a president, people gather to read—what? Not stories. Not articles or plays. They read poems.

I think the reason is partly because poems are so intimate. Often we write poems for personal reasons. A girl likes a boy, writes him a love poem, and slips it into his backpack where she knows he will find it.

It has been said that writing a poem for someone else is like giving blood because it comes from the heart of the writer and goes to the heart of the receiver. Poems are filled with words from the heart.

The power of poetry comes at least partly from its brevity. Poems are short, and they pack a punch—often they say a lot with a few well-chosen words. Here's a poem I recently wrote:

Forget-Me-Not

I left one flower
on Grandma's coffin:
a forget-me-not
as if I could

Of course, not everybody is a fan of poetry. I often run into kids who don't like to write poems. "Poems are boring," one girl muttered when I visited her classroom. She complained that her teacher had spent hour after hour dissecting poems and pulling out similes, metaphors, and symbolism.

"If I had one wish," she told me, "it would be that I'd never have to analyze another poem for the rest of my life."

She's got her wish, at least in this book. This book is about writing poetry, not analyzing it. I wrote this book to help you write poems and to give practical ideas for making your poems sound the way you want them to sound. We're not going to smash poems up into the tiniest pieces. But I do think it's helpful to be wide awake when you write a poem. Lots of poets—both kids and grown-ups—fall into a trap. They view a poem as a one-hundred-yard sprint. They dash off the poem in one fast draft and make a quick decision whether it's good or not. If it's good, they keep it. If it stinks, they throw it away. Many poets never think about how they're writing the poem, where it works, and where it needs more work. Big mistake.

I wrote this book to help you think deeper about how you can make your poem shine. You might be surprised to find that I don't approach poetry the way many teachers do, by looking at poetry forms: haiku, couplets, diamante, acrostics, limericks, etc. Some writers like to start with a preset form, but I think of that as writing the poem from the outside in. I have written a chapter on the uses (and abuses) of form. But in this book I focus on helping you write the poem *from the inside out.*

We'll start with the heart, the guts, the feel of

poetry. The three pillars of poetry are emotion, image, and music. We'll explore those elements in the first three chapters. Later on we'll look at ways you can refine the poem by using "white spaces," cutting unnecessary words, and sharpening the ending. After that we'll explore different ways you can have fun by going public with your poetry.

Whenever I visit schools I meet lots of kids who like writing poems as much as I do.

"They're short and intense," Andy, a seventh grader, told me. "When you're writing a poem you can see right away whether or not it's going to get off the ground." I like Andy's description of a poem getting off the ground. He thinks like a poet!

I will never be able to fly like a hawk or dunk a basketball like Kobe Bryant. But with words and poems I have been able to achieve that sense of perfection. It doesn't happen all the time. Sometimes it happens for only a fleeting moment—but it does happen, and it's as exhilarating as flight. I got that feeling when I wrote these lines about the coming of the dawn:

Dawn picks
bits of dark
from between
the blades of grass . . .

Have you ever seen those "complete taco dinners" that come in a box? The idea is that you get just about everything you need: taco shells, taco sauce, sauce for the meat, etc. No, this book does not try to be a "poem in the box." But you'll find some great stuff for making your poems sing.

Recently I worked with a group of fourth graders and, later, a group of sixth graders. In both classes we wrote poetry together. We had only twenty-five minutes for the actual writing. The students' poems weren't perfect, of course, but every one of them had something wonderful in it. I want this book to help you have more of those moments in the poetry you write. I want you to feel the power of poetry. It's my hope that through this book you will discover lots of ways to make your poems shine, sing, soar.

ONE

An Emotional X-ray

What poetry does at its very best is to make the reader feel. Feel deeply and truly.

—JANE YOLEN

Poetry saved my life. Well, maybe that's a bit of an exaggeration, but poetry saved my emotional life. And without emotions, what's life worth anyway?

In 1974 my brother Bob got killed in a car accident. He was seventeen years old, the fifth in our family of nine children, and his death tore up everyone in my family. Bob's death stirred up a hornets' nest of emotions inside me: anger, grief, guilt—even some bitterness. I could feel that swarm of feelings buzzing in my chest day and night. I needed some kind of container to hold all of them.

Poetry became that container. After Bobby's death I read lots of poems. I liked poems because they were short and potent. Some of them really packed a wallop while others, like the following poem, felt like soothing medicine poured over my wound:

The Milkweed
by Richard Wilbur

Anonymous as cherubs
Over the crib of God
White seeds are floating
Out of my burst pod.

What power had I
Before I learned to yield?
Shatter me, great wind:
I shall possess the field.

This poem really touched me. I was awed and

somehow encouraged by the idea that the milk-weed can only spread *after* it has been shattered by the wind. I had been shattered by my brother's death. Maybe there was hope for me, too. This poem gave me the courage to go on with my life.

I read zillions of poems around that time, and I wrote lots of poems, too. A poem is like an X-ray of what's going on inside you. Inevitably, most of the poems I wrote were reflections on or reactions to Bobby's death. My parents published a small "Bobby Book," and in it was a poem I wrote that was a letter addressed to my brother. It's a long poem that ends with these lines:

> Let's play a game, Bob:
> we'll be the pieces
> and you be the glue.
> I understand that your way is quietly.

When you write this kind of poetry, it almost doesn't matter whether it is "good" or not. The important thing is that it's good for the soul. I can see now that writing that poem was the beginning of my healing process.

Poems convey strong feelings. You get a little

"thump" in your heart when you read them. That thump comes partly because poems aren't afraid to tell the truth. Poetry can be utterly honest. Listen to this poem by Linley Hallmark, a fourth grader in Alabama. She wrote this poem as a tribute to her teacher Ann Marie Corgill, and you can feel the emotion pouring from each line:

The Magic of Life Experience

You're the one each child dreams
of becoming.
You're the one they look up to.
You're the one who taught us how
to reach for our dreams…
all 21 of us.
You taught us to love one another,
work with each other,
and make us feel good about the
person we really are.
You gave us power and courage to
go on with the rest of our life.
And most of all you gave us
a wonderful year of life experience.

Poems are the "daredevils" of writing because a poem will say what nobody else wants to say. Poems speak the unspeakable, and often it's this honest quality that makes a poem impossible to put down. Megan Daily, a fourth grader in Alabama, wrote the following poem:

Divorce

Parents together
They love each other
Then they split

Like the wrong ends of a magnet put together
Or like a passenger fleeing from a
Sinking ship
Like a young bird leaving its nest
Like a picture ripped in half

Like a man leaving a woman for a better one.

Some people find it natural to be honest in their poetry; for other people it is much harder. It can be difficult to be honest in a poem because sometimes it's hard to be honest with yourself. Often I write a few lines of poetry, but when I reread them they sound "canned," like the fake sentiment in a greeting card. The lines don't ring true. When a line sounds false, I know I'm not getting to the heart of the feeling. Here are a few ideas for dealing with this problem:

Think of a poem as an X-ray. Just as an X-ray penetrates to examine the bones inside your body, a poem can probe the "bones" of your inner being.

Try "poem-speak." Speak to someone inside the poem. In Linley Hallmark's poem, the emotion comes partly from the way she is speaking to her teacher. Poem-speak is different from life-speak: Linley probably wouldn't speak with such feeling or sincerity in real life. Poem-speak is like condensed milk, which is made thicker and sweeter when the water is removed.

Convey feelings through images. Poets carefully select objects or images for their poems. If you pick the right ones, you don't have to use the word for the feeling you're trying to get across to the reader. The following poem was written by Matthew Oh, a fifth grader in New York:

My Mom

My mom takes good care of me.
She's the gardener,
I'm the rose,
she waters me every day.
When it gets cold
she puts me in a pot
and brings me inside.

When you read Matthew's poem you feel the love for his mother shining through, but you notice that he never uses that word. Instead, he compares a mother caring for a child to a gardener tending a rose. This comparison is simple and very effective.

Don't say too much. I read many poems that go on too long. The power in the poem gets diluted in too many adjectives and images. If you are reading this book, I'm sure you can write long, involved stories. But "long and involved" may work against the power of what you want to say. Think small.

The following poem was written by Billy Baker, a seventh grader who lives in North Carolina. When Billy wrote to me he said: "I am Dislexic so words are not my best friend. But I can make poems O.K." He wrote this poem after his dog Shelby died. After I read this poem I disagreed with Billy: I think his poems are more than "O.K."—he uses language very well. Look at how much emotion he can generate using only thirty-six words.

Shelby's Star

When I look up in the sky
I don't see the star I used to see.
Where did you go?
The most beautiful star.
Maybe Shelby took it with her
when she went away.

I miss Shelby.

TWO

Image

Poems are other people's snapshots in which we see our own lives.

—CHARLES SIMIC

A few years ago I was reading my poetry book *Water Planet* to my son Robert. He was about five years old at the time.

"Did you make the words *and* the pictures?" he asked me.

I laughed. *Water Planet* contains about thirty poems, but there is not a single illustration in the book!

The pictures Robert saw in his head were created

by words. Mental pictures, or images, are at the heart of poetry, just like emotions. Think back to the last chapter, when we read that memorable line in Megan's poem "Divorce": *Like the wrong ends of a magnet put together.* Because we have all held magnets, and felt this strange repelling force, Megan's image gives us a physical sense of two things pushing away from each other. It is an image we can *feel.*

Remember Matthew's poem in Chapter 1, "My Mom," where he writes: *She waters me every day.* Matthew mentions something we have all done— watering a plant—but this familiar image gives his poem depth and heart. In this chapter we'll look closely at images—what they are and how you create them in your own poetry.

An image is like a picture. If you want to create strong images, get in the habit of observing the world so you can create your own pictures using words. Pay attention. Be alive to what's going on around you, as well as inside you, because both will provide you with images for your poems.

Observing the world starts with taking a deep breath. This can be hard to do. Slow down. The painter Georgia O'Keeffe once said: "Nobody sees a flower, really—it is too small—we haven't time, and to see takes time, like to have a friend takes time."

Once you slow down, you'll discover that you have powerful tools—your five senses—to capture the world around you.

Look. Our sunflowers were tall and proud in August when they first blossomed. But now in September their heads are drooping. As a poet, you want to get in the habit of noticing things like that. For example, study the way light and shadow dance together in the forest. When you walk in that forest it almost seems like being underwater.

Listen. When I wake up I like to lie in bed, listening. The birds outside my house are loudest at dawn. Soon my sons wake up, and I can hear them laughing together in their bedroom. One time while I was listening to them the thought occurred to me that their laughter was a language of its own, a language only they could speak.

Smell. Notice how your school has that ultra-clean, almost antiseptic smell on Monday morning.

Touch. Let your fingers feel the difference

between a smooth, finished desktop or tabletop and the rougher, unfinished wood underneath.

Taste. Savor the tangy sweetness of a single raspberry. Notice how the air tastes different after a rainstorm.

Observations like these will feed your poetry by training you to be specific and detailed. The poet Charles Simic reminds us that a poem is a "snapshot," not a video. You might begin by describing a single image in your head. Close your eyes. What do you see? Don't worry about whether or not it looks like a perfectly composed poem. Chances are it won't. Just write down the image, as I did here:

> my old dog sleeps in the kitchen
> lying against the side of the stove
> the warmest place in the house

This sounds like the start of a poem. Georgia Heard, a poet and friend of mine, says that the challenge is to describe something as if we're seeing it for the first time. Look at this poem by Kristine O'Connell George:

Polliwogs

Come see
What I found!
Chubby commas,
Mouths Round,
Plump babies,
Stubby as toes.
Polliwogs!
Tadpoles!

Come see
What I found!
Frogs-in-waiting—
Huddled in puddles,
Snuggled in mud.

Chubby commas! Whoa—I wish I'd written that! I also love all the short *uh* sounds in the last two lines. Kristine O'Connell George brings a freshness to her subject, as if she has seen polliwogs for the very first time. She creates a surprising image by relating two things—tadpoles and commas— that at first don't seem as if they should be compared. It's a surprising connection, which makes it effective. If you relate two things using "like" or "as" it is called a *simile*. If the comparison is implied without those words, as in the polliwog poem, it is called a *metaphor*. You probably already know all this, but I figured I should mention it anyway.

John Capobianco, a student in New York, uses two lovely metaphors in the following poem he wrote about his shoes. This terrific poem reminds me that a poem doesn't have to be long and complicated to do its job.

My Shoes

My shoes are a home
for my feet.

The five toes are brothers
sitting by the fire.

A poem like this a wake-up call. When you incorporate images like these into a poem, you help us to see the tired old world in a brand-new way. By doing this you give something back to the world.

I try to bring "new eyes" to everything that comes across my path during the day. The poems from my book *Ordinary Things* germinated from the things I noticed on the four-mile walks I took every afternoon after I finished writing. During those walks I tried to clear my head and notice the details of the landscape—the dogs at one old house that barked at me and looked as if they wanted attention. Freshly cut firewood, and the piles of powdery sawdust below. I returned from these walks, took out my writer's notebook, and jotted down what had struck me. In one yard I had noticed the clothes hanging from the clothes-line. The breeze would blow the clothes and make them change shape. This gave me an idea for the following poem:

Clothesline

There's an orange towel and
two white t-shirts pinned
at the waist all trying to

dry themselves in the
breeze.

Filled with air the two t-shirts
puff up with sudden bodies
real and muscular which
vanish when the wind
dies.

The wind lifts the towel until
it lies horizontal as if trying
to screw up the nerve
to let go and
fly

For me, the challenge is to describe an image, but to do it in a way that incorporates a little surprise, a twist, like the barb on a hook that makes it stick, makes it go in deeper. There are many ways of building surprise into your poem.

In one class I visited, a boy named Brian wrote a poem about his mother baking cookies. The last line of his poem read, "Even the house smells happy." I read another poem by a young poet who wrote, "the sky holds the earth in its arms."

Nice! I had never thought of describing earth and sky in this way. In this wonderful image, something inanimate (sky) is given human characteristics (arms). I encourage you to try this in your own poem—describing the trees in winter standing at attention, for instance, or pointing dark, bony hands at each other. The fancy name for this technique is *personification*, but it's more important that you learn how to do this than memorize the name for it.

Symbols give you another way to use imagery in your poetry. The eagle on a dollar bill is a symbol for freedom. In a poem, a symbol is a real thing or object that stands for something else. In Robert Frost's famous poem "The Road Not Taken," for example, the two paths are symbols of decisions we all make in our lives.

You might also try to mix things up and keep the reader off balance by playing with different kinds of images in the same poem. I have been working on a collection of flower poems. In the following poem, I describe a water lily by letting the flower speak for itself. This poem contrasts two different ways of looking at the water lily. There is a tension between these images—pure and beautiful vs. nitty-gritty—that makes the poem fun to read:

Water Lily

I am famous: the sacred lotus,
a symbol of grace and purity,

   though to croaking frogs I'm no more
   than a hang-out joint, an all-night store.

My petals enfold stamens of gold.
I float, serene, while down below

   these roots of mine are deeply stuck
   in the coolest most delicious muck.

THREE

Fresh Music

That spools the wind into merciless frenzies,
And drives the rain like cannon fire,
And paints the clouds in shades of corpses,
And splits the sky with tentacles of fire,
And virulent roars that shatter the night . . .

—TOM FLETCHER
FROM *"Falling Through the Earth"*

One time I visited a class of little kids in New York City and read them some poems. The poems weren't humorous, so I was surprised when the kids giggled after each poem I read.

"Why are you laughing?" I asked.

"The poems sound funny," one boy said.

"Funny how?"

"It's like you're at a party," he explained, "and you hear some fresh music, and you want to get up and dance."

Well said! In fact, I would put poetry closer to music than to other kinds of writing. Like our favorite songs, poems have rhythms, cadences, and sounds that burrow deep inside us and become a permanent part of who we are. In this chapter we'll look at four ways you can infuse your poems with music.

1) Play with the sound of words. I grew up near the ocean, in Marshfield, Massachusetts. I loved going to the beach, riding the waves, or just hanging out with my brothers in the shallow surf. It was a blast, floating there, getting knocked this way and that by the small waves that had already broken and were rolling in. Recently I started working on a book of beach poems, and I tried to capture that feeling in this poem:

Wallowing

we walk on our hands
and laze in shallow surf

like a bunch of sea sloths
or slow motion manatees

no place to go
no hurry to get there

wubbling with the bubbles
foaming with the froth

in the noisy crumble tumble
of the ragamuffin waves

You'll notice several things about this poem:

• I don't use any capital letters, or punctuation either. I wanted the language to be free-flowing, just like the lazy waves or the feeling I'm trying to communicate. This is called *poetic license*, and it's a lot of fun. In school we learn the rules of language: how to write a complete sentence, use a topic sentence, not use fragments, etc. These rules are important, but when you write a poem you can break those rules to create the effect you want.

• True, the lines of each stanza don't rhyme, but I rhyme words in several of the lines: *crumble* and *tumble, wubbling* with the *bubbles*. This is called *internal rhyme*.

• There's a separate rhythm to the last four lines of the poem. Say them aloud and you'll hear it. I hear two main beats in each of the lines:

> <u>wub</u>bling with the <u>bub</u>bles
> <u>foam</u>ing with the <u>froth</u>
> in the <u>noi</u>sy crumble <u>tum</u>ble
> of the <u>ra</u>gamuffin <u>waves</u>

• The poem plays with the meanings of words. The dictionary tells us that *ragamuffin* means a dirty, ragged person, which has nothing to do with waves. I knew that the meaning doesn't exactly fit here, but so what? I have always loved the sound of that word, and it didn't seem like too much of a stretch to use it here to describe the wild, unkempt, disorderly waves. *Wubbling*, of course, isn't a word at all, but it sounded like a good way to describe how we were hanging out with the waves. (Hint: Yes, you can invent a new word to fit your poem!)

2) Have fun with alliteration. You can make your poetry more musical by repeating the beginning consonants of certain words within a line. This is called *alliteration*. In this snippet of one of my poems, you can hear the *H* sounds repeated in the second line:

> The trees were immense and silent,
> hiding us under huge hushed skirts.

I used this technique toward the end of another poem:

When The Roses Revolted

> The roses were fed up.
> They were sick sick sick
> of being symbols for love.

One night they revolted,
crept out of flower shops,
jumped out of windows
and touched the dirt!

They spent that night
drinking real night air,
carousing with clover,
boogying with bluebells,
dancing with dandelions,
and in this way they
rediscovered their
roots.

In each of the lines—*carousing with clover //
boogying with bluebells // dancing with dandelions*—
you can hear the repetition of the consonant
sounds that begin the important words. I think
these are the best lines of the poem.

I encourage you to experiment with alliteration in your own poems. See what happens when
you repeat the initial consonants of words in a particular line. You may find that alliteration makes a
line more musical and more fun to say out loud.

3) Fine-tune the rhythm. For Father's Day my son Robert wrote me this poem. Robert is in fourth grade.

A Poem

This is a poem about a poem of
a little boy who was writing a poem
and in this poem was a little boy
who was writing a poem for his dad.
The poem was about how the boy wanted to
thank his dad for what he had done.

I was delighted by the gift of this quirky poem. Although the poem doesn't rhyme, there's a nice rhythm in the first four lines. If you reread this poem out loud, tapping your hand on your leg, I think you'll find that there are four beats in each of the first three lines and three beats in the fourth line, like this:

This is a poem about a poem of
a little boy who was writing a poem

and <u>in</u> this p<u>o</u>em was a <u>little</u> b<u>oy</u>
who was <u>writ</u>ing a p<u>o</u>em for his <u>dad</u>.

In many poems the music comes out through the rhythm, or beat. There are lots of different kinds of beats. William Shakespeare wrote his plays in iambic pentameter—ten syllables per line. You can look at a copy of any one of his plays, open to almost any page, and when you count the syllables in one line there are always ten. Amazing! Iambic pentameter has a rhythm that reflects the beating of the human heart.

Poetic rhythm can get pretty complicated, and it includes some weird-sounding terms like *trochees*, *anapests*, *dactyls*, *iambs*, and *spondees*. In this book, I'm not going to explore all those terms, but I want to encourage you to start tuning your ear to the rhythm in poetry.

Rhyming poems often contain a strong, regular rhythm. But if you read a poem out loud, you can often hear the rhythm in unrhymed poems, as in the poem Robert wrote for me. The following untitled poem was written by Natalia M. Belting. Read this poem out loud (in a soft voice if you are in school) and listen to its rhythm, especially in the first half of the poem:

> The dark gray clouds,
> the great gray clouds,
> the black rolling clouds are elephants
> going down to the sea for water.
> They draw up the water in their trunks.
> They march back again across the sky.
> They spray the earth again with the water,
> and men say it is raining.

As you start to write your poem, close your eyes and say the words aloud. Listen to the rhythm of the words as you write them down. When you finish your poem, reread it several times, listening to how it sounds. Sometimes the rhythm is off—it sounds clunky, and you have to change or even remove words until the poem has the music you want it to have.

4) Use repetition for emphasis. Kailie West, a fourth grader, was working on a poem about her pet Labrador. She began like this:

I've been thinking about my old old dog
He walks across the floor with a thump thump
thump

When Kailie writes *thump thump thump* she lets us hear the dog's belabored gait as he walks across the floor. The repetition here creates a particular rhythm in each of these lines. But it does something else, too. By repeating the words *old* and *thump,* Kailie asks the reader to linger at these important parts of the poem. The repetition emphasizes the word *old* in the first line and deepens the emotion of the poem. Repetition is an important glue you can use to hold a poem together, and I encourage you to experiment with it. Do you have an important line, a certain part of the poem you want to stay in the ear of the reader? If so, try repeating that part. You can repeat a word or phrase. You might repeat a particular line, like a chorus in a song. Or you might have the final line in a poem echo the very first line. Andrew Ammerman, a Connecticut fifth grader, uses repetition to great effect in the following poem:

Little Old Me

Little old me
stuck in the middle
With a nasty old sister
And an annoying little brother

Little old me
Big but small
Growing too fast
So I get my old sister's stuff
But give it to my little brother

Little old me
Gets picked on and annoyed
So old, but so young
Little old me stuck in the middle

FOUR

Interview with Kristine O'Connell George

Kristine O'Connell George has written a number of award-winning poetry collections for young readers. Her books include The Great Frog Race and Other Poems; Old Elm Speaks: Tree Poems; *and* Little Dog Poems. *I admire the way she can create beautiful images with only a few words. Listen to her wise words on writing.*

Why do you write? I mean, what's in it for you?

I write because I enjoy the challenge of capturing an elusive image on paper, or finding just the perfect word or form for a poem. That's much more important than the possibility that something I've written might be published. For that reason I'll probably keep pushing myself to try new kinds of writing. I enjoy the private satisfaction of making a piece as good as I possibly can and developing an idea—watching it grow and take on new substance and depth. I'm intrigued and sometimes startled by those times when an idea somehow takes on a life of its own, surprises me, or gives me new insight.

Where do you get your ideas?

For a long time I thought my ideas lived in the medicine cabinet in my bathroom. It seemed as if each time I took out my toothbrush and toothpaste I'd get an idea—or a phrase or concept I'd been searching for would suddenly be swimming around in my head. Lately, however, my ideas seem to be located on the back patio, where I like to sit with my feet up and watch my weeds grow. Many of my best ideas arrive when I'm not actively thinking about writing and am simply paying attention to the world around me.

I also get ideas when I'm reading. This is not about copying other people's work—it's about what happens when I immerse myself in language and ideas. Often when I do that my own feelings/thoughts/ideas bob up to the surface.

What sorts of prewriting/brainstorming do you find helpful?

I try to keep a notebook, but I also have a very bad habit of scribbling things down on pieces of paper all over the house and in my car. My family is trained not to throw anything away, because sometimes I'll have written a single word on a bill, and that word is a key to an idea I'm thinking about. I'll brainstorm ideas in my notebook, but I never discuss what I'm working on with anyone. For some reason, talking seems to sap my energy and enthusiasm for an idea or project.

Many writers find it hard to begin writing. Do you? How do you start?

I just start. And keep going.

When do you write? Do you stick to a regular schedule?

I try and write during school hours when my daughter is gone and the house is quiet. However, I'm definitely a night owl and if I'm excited about a project and it's going well, I'll work very late at night. It's not unusual for me to finally turn the light off in my office at 2 A.M.

Do you ever run into writer's block?

I'm constantly raising the high bar on myself and setting new challenges. Sometimes I'll get very frustrated and am certain that I can be more creative or that I need to find something wholly original to tackle. At that point, it's best for me to go for a hike, read a favorite author, or simply put my project away for a few days. Doing something physical like digging holes or pulling weeds helps, too.

What sorts of revisions do you typically do?

I enjoy revising, and revise extensively. Sometimes, for me, the trick is to not overrevise to the point that I dampen or extinguish the thought that originally sparked the poem. I always record my poems (sometimes my prose too) on a tape recorder and listen to what I've written. Then I'll listen to the tape in the car or where there are few distractions. This helps me hear the poem, and often I'll make small changes—even small ones like a comma—based on how it sounds when it's read out loud.

Is your editor an important part of your process?

Yes. Sometimes there is a certain point with a piece or poem when I'm unable to see it objectively. That's when I welcome and most value the editing process and the give-and-take of hearing a second opinion. I don't always agree with editorial suggestions, but I always listen and give them careful consideration. I try to step back and see my work through someone else's eyes. My best editing experiences are those when a question or comment helps me move the poem to another level and make it significantly better. That's a great feeling!

Do you have any advice for young writers?

Write because you love to write or have something you want to say. Learn to honor the process rather than the final product. How *you* feel about your words, thoughts, and ideas is far more important than getting published. Don't look at events in your life as fodder for your writing to the point that you're not fully present in the moment. Don't be like the tourist who spends so much time behind the lens of a camera that he misses the big picture.

Everyone says READ, and that is the best advice I've ever been given. The creative process is elusive, and it often takes years to discover the best way to work and to be able to consistently tap that part of your mind. Think of your mind as having different radio frequencies—you need to "tune in" to the right frequency to write creatively. Reading is an excellent way to tune your mind to the writing frequency.

FIVE

Poem Sparks:
What to Write About

Look for the poetry that grows under your feet.
—RAINER MARIE RILKE

Last spring I planted sunflower seeds. We got a lot of rain, and two weeks later tiny shoots had poked through the dirt. All summer I watched them gradually inch up until some of the stalks were tall as a man. It wasn't until mid-August that the first blossom, a miniature sun, opened up.

Some things grow like that—slowly—but not everything does. Try this: The next summer day you get rain followed by warm, humid weather, go out into the woods. You'll be amazed at all the mushrooms and toadstools that have sprouted up overnight. They don't grow gradually. If the conditions are right—POOF!—they suddenly appear as if by magic.

If you want to write a poem, you need something to write about. You may be lucky enough to find that ideas for poems simply appear to you the way those mushrooms appear in the forest. It has happened to me. One morning I woke up and found that my head was crammed full of ideas for love poems. Lots of them. After breakfast I sat down to write. The thirty-three poems came easily, and I barely even had to revise them. In three weeks I finished my book *I Am Wings: Poems About Love.*

Unfortunately, it doesn't always work like that. If you are like me, you will go through periods when your poetry well has run dry. Don't despair. Check the following places if you are looking for something to write about.

Concerns of the heart. I have found that my best poetry ideas are things that concern me deeply. It's not so much that I choose them—they choose me. These ideas grab me by the sleeve. They insist: Write about me! Now! And they don't let go until I do.

A few years ago my mother had heart bypass surgery, and of course I was terribly worried. I knew enough about heart surgery to know that doctors have to stop the heart so they can work on it while it's not beating. On the morning of her surgery I was doing housework, when a sentence—*Today Mom's heart is stopped*—popped into my head. This sentence froze my own blood. Here's the poem I wrote about it:

Today My Mother's Heart Is Stopped

Today my mother's heart is stopped.
The world's first true sound, my first
music, the steady metronome that
rocked me inside her womb—stopped.

Today my mother's heart is stopped
so the surgeon can hold it in his hands,
and I cannot find any air to breathe.

A thousand miles away from her
I hang clean towels on a line.
The sheets flash in the light.
As a boy I played in the sandbox
and watched her lift on her tiptoes,
pinning our clothes onto the line.
Later I helped her take them in,
and in my arms they smelled
sweet like sky, like sun,
like summer,
mother.

What you see. My son Robert Fletcher wrote this
in fourth grade:

Water

When you look into water do you
see yourself in the reflection
or do you see a
place where life flows through
like sun flows through a
window on a hot summer day?

Do you see something
that gives life to every thing
in the world, or do you see a
place to go swimming?

This poem demonstrates that you don't have to go to an exotic place like Fiji or Maui to capture an image or idea. People have written poems while in solitary confinement. Look at your own world, the bluish veins on Grandma's hands, the devilish look on a baby's face. There is poetry everywhere.

What you wonder about. In my book *A Writer's Notebook*, I wrote a chapter on "fierce wonderings" and "bottomless questions." These are the kinds of haunting questions you can live and ponder but never really answer. Not surprisingly, these "wonder-full" questions provide great grist for poems.

Julia Salem, an elementary school student in New Jersey, wrote about the death of her mother in a series of poems. In one striking poem the lines are long and ragged, as if they haven't yet found their shape. This uneven form seems appropriate, since the author is still trying to sort out this event. Here she asks herself a number of tough questions:

**The rope of frustration is swinging
in my mind.**

I think of myself absorbed in figuring out
the meaning of forever. My own difficulties,
they strangle me, when will I realize who I
am? I feel my words waiting to come out,
I remind myself not to talk the ways I'd like
to. No one could have a bolder imitation
of myself. Could my feelings deceive me?
Could someone push me into the cold sand?
I think of myself as my own friend, I talk,
I tangle up in my mixed-up head. Am I me?
It's hard to work, for me it's harder to play.

There's an infinite list of poetry ideas available
to everyone. Memories, reflections, dreams, fan-
tasies, odd facts—any of these things might spark
a poem. And don't forget to study the subjects
other poets choose. All the poems in this book are
invitations. I hope they unlock a door and invite

you to try a similar poem of your own.

Be careful, however, if you are writing a poem about a familiar topic: spring, God, sunset. These topics have been done and done and, in some cases, made into greeting cards! That's not to say avoid them completely, but make sure you have a fresh angle.

Concerns about the world. In one famous poem, Langston Hughes wondered about "what happens to a dream deferred." Are you outraged by the pollution of our rivers? The melting of the ice caps? The genocide of the Great Plains Indians? Write about it. A poem is a way for you to speak against the injustice of the world. When you write such a poem, you join thousands of writers from all around the world who have written poems to speak for the powerless, who have tried through poetry to make this world a better place.

The catalyst for this kind of poem can come from a newspaper article, a TV news show, or something you witness yourself. Patricia Clark, a poet and teacher, once visited a museum where she saw a bill of sale for a slave girl. She was appalled by this piece of paper, which detailed how a human being could be bought and sold like a horse, a bushel of wheat, or a piece of furniture. It sparked her to write a poem.

Political or activist poems are important. But when I write this kind of poem, I try to keep in mind some words of caution the writer Richard Price gave me when I studied writing with him: *If you want to send a message go to Western Union.* In other words, it's okay to be passionate about what you believe in, but beware of lecturing at your audience. That sort of preachy writing will turn readers off in a heartbeat. The best poems don't tell us what to think, they *show* us, and they let us feel it, too.

The following poem was written by my brother Tom Fletcher. I admire the precise imagery that captures a moment in time. It seems to me that in the final four lines Tom describes the job of the poet.

The Wild Flight

The moon's lean crescent
vaguely illuminated an open field
and black forest outline behind.

Neck tucked, an eerie shriek,
a tall buck,
hiding in the stealthy weeds,
exploded from its knees,
out and upward
in one great scissoring spasm,
pounding field under itself
in furious silence.
A streak of wild earth,
the weight of a large man,
its coat of arms,
tan with white lines,
glowed in the moonlight,
surreal and magnificent.

I spend days gathering images,
the night in reconstruction,
sewing dreams like patches
along the seams of a diminishing world.

PART TWO

Nurturing the Flame

My friend isn't unusual. My experience is that most people don't consciously craft a poem as they write it. Most people seem to think that writing a poem is like emotional oil gushing from the soul, an expression of our deepest selves. It may start that way. But crude oil is called crude because it has to be refined. Over the years I have learned several strategies for crafting the raw materials of a poem. They have made me a much better poet, and in this chapter I'll share them with you. Keep in mind the three poetry pillars—emotion, image, and music—as we take a look at ways you can craft your poem from the inside out.

Think fragments. It's a funny thing. For years, teachers drill the Rules Of Language into your head. Use complete sentences! Begin each sentence with a capital letter! Don't begin a sentence with "and" or "but." No fragments. Certain teachers have been known to inflict pain (or at least low grades) on students who forget to follow these rules.

But a poem is an impressionistic piece of writing, a word painting in which the writer tries to capture a moment, an image. Fragments can work like a dab of color to bring your word painting alive. The following poem was written by Michael Wright, a fourth grader from Oklahoma. He wrote this while visiting New York City for the first time:

The Subway

People everywhere,
Pushing, shoving,
Packed in like sardines,
Can't hardly breathe—

GOING CRAZY!!!!!

Michael's fragments help to convey the energy and the sharp sensory details of the subway. Think how different this poem would sound if Michael had written it in complete sentences:

There are people everywhere,
Pushing and shoving.
We are packed in like sardines.
We can't hardly breathe.

I'M GOING CRAZY!!!!!

The fragments Michael used do a much better job of conveying the loud, wild, helter-skelter world of the subway.

Consider the shape. When you're writing a story, you don't have to think about how it looks on the page. You simply go to the first line, indent, begin writing, and continue until you fill up the page. Poems are different. Writing a poem is like building a word house. Do you want your house to be wide, with lots of words on each line? Or tall and skinny, with just a few words on each line? Many poets like to play with shape as a way to convey the meaning of the poem. For example, a poem about someone falling might end with a word that looks like it has fallen far below the others. This is called concrete poetry. Here's a poem by Emily Ellington, a Connecticut sixth grader.

Soda

Fiz tickles
my tongue

Coldness
trickles
up
my spine
like the
last drops
trickle into
my mouth

               My taste buds

want to
savor
more
of the
sweet
carbonated
liquid

Bubbles
                hop
around like
Mexican jumping beans

My

            certain

drink

            is

a dark
brown
not
crystal clear

Sugar enters
my body
causing me
to bounce
off the walls

I can't get enough
of the

            fizzy
            sweet

bubbly

            carbonated

liquid

my

        body

craves

        more

I

        can't

resist

        the

craving

I invite you to go back and reread Emily's poem. Ask yourself why she chose to write it the way she did. Read the poem aloud. Does the shape affect the way it sounds when you read it? This poem would have had a much different feel if she had written it in long, dense lines with lots of words. Emily has devised a shape in which the words themselves look carbonated.

Experiment with line breaks. In a story or report, the unit of thought is a sentence. But in a poem, the unit of thought is the line. By "line," I mean the words you write on one line of a poem. Your poem will change—both in meaning and in sound—depending on which words you place on any particular line.

In a story the sentences are organized into paragraphs. In a poem, you organize the lines into *stanzas*. *Stanza* means "room" in Italian. Just as each room in a house has different purposes, each stanza in a poem conveys a different idea.

Often you write what *sounds* like a poem but *looks* more like a story. With a rhyming poem, line breaks are usually easy. You simply break the line after the rhyming word. With a free verse poem it's a little trickier. Here are some ideas on how to create line breaks. We'll work with "Waiting for the Splash," one of the poems from my book *I Am Wings: Poems About Love*.

Last night after you hung up I wrote you a poem hoping it might change your heart. This morning I tell myself: Get serious, man. Someone once compared writing a poem and hoping it will change the world to dropping rose petals down a deep well, waiting for the splash.

Read the poem out loud and listen for those

places where there is a natural pause. For example, when I read it out loud my voice wants to pause after *Last night*. I put two slash marks at this place. The double slash marks tell me that when the poem gets rewritten the words after this mark (in this case *after you hung up*) will be a new line. Continue making slash marks throughout this passage. Here's what I came up with:

> Last night // after you hung up // I wrote you a poem // hoping it might // change your heart. // This morning // I tell myself: // Get serious, man. // Someone once compared // writing a poem // and hoping it will // change the world // to dropping rose petals // down a deep well, // waiting for the splash.

The finished poem looks like this:

> Last night
> after you hung up
> I wrote you a poem
> hoping it might
> change your heart.

This morning
I tell myself:
Get serious, man.
Someone once compared
writing a poem
and hoping it will
change the world
to dropping rose petals
down a deep well

waiting for the splash.

After you divide your poem into line breaks, you'll want to read it aloud again to make sure it looks and sounds the way you want it. The words on each line should suggest a single image. If the words convey more than one image, that's usually a clue that you need to break the line into two lines.

Also, think about the sound of the line. When you read a poem, there is a brief pause at the end of each line. For this reason, poems with shorter lines, like "Waiting for the Splash," tend to be read slowly. Poems with longer lines tend to build up more momentum and velocity. You can hear that momentum of words in "Song of Myself," a poem by Walt Whitman. Here is an excerpt from that long poem:

> Alone far in the wilds and mountains I hunt,
> Wandering amazed at my lightness and glee,
> In the late afternoon choosing a safe spot to
>   pass the night,
> Kindling a fire and broiling the fresh-kill'd
>   game,
> Falling asleep on the gather'd leaves with my
>   dog and gun by my side.

Don't get frustrated with line breaks. Remember: there is more than one way to do it. You might try writing two or three versions of the poem with various kinds of line breaks before you settle on what looks, sounds, and feels right.

Use white spaces. Have you ever gone to a fancy restaurant or eaten a super-elegant seven-course dinner at a wedding? Between a fish and a meat course they will serve a small dish of sherbet. When I ate a meal like this my first reaction was: Why are they serving dessert in the middle of the meal? My father explained that the idea is to "cleanse your palate"—in other words, to remove the taste of the dish you've just eaten so you can enjoy what's to come.

That's how white spaces work in a poem. A white space is a blank line in the poem: no words, nothing. By inserting a white space instead of a line of text, you build in a pause, a moment of silence. This allows your reader to take a breath and get ready for the part of the poem that will follow. I've noticed how often a wonderful line or image can get buried in a dense part of the poem. By using a white space, you make sure that image doesn't get lost.

The following poem is about a boy, my brother's friend, who drowned while I was in high school. There is an important line near the end. I didn't want it to get lost so I put a white space before and after it:

Where John Curtain Drowned

He was a tall kid,
a magician on the basketball court.
He could dribble with both hands.

I once saw him make a shot
from half court, perfect swish,
but he never learned to swim.

On my brother's boat
we sail past the spot
where John Curtain drowned.

No buoy, no marker, nothing.

When we get closer
I stop talking

I hold my breath

and don't breathe again
til we've sailed safely past.

End with a bang. Endings matter a lot. The final image, line, or idea in a poem will be the one freshest in the reader's mind when he or she finishes reading. What do you want to leave readers with? I read a lot of poems that have some great lines but end weakly. Or often a poem has a great line in the middle but goes on too long.

Here's what I do. First I write a rough draft of the poem. I know it's not perfect, but I want to get down as much of it as possible. I reread the poem and put a star next to my best line. I try to revise the poem so that it ends on the best line. This strategy may seem formulaic, but it has been a consistent winner for me.

In my book *Relatively Speaking: Poems About Family*, there is a poem about the new baby in the house. All the relatives make comments about who the baby looks like. Read the poem, and check out the ending. I think I ended with my best line. And you'll notice that the last line is preceded by white space.

New Baby

Soon as the baby gets born
before she's two hours old
people start dividing her up

"She has Daddy's big ears"
"Got Grandma's double chin"
"She has my olive eyes"

like she's just a bunch
of borrowed parts
stitched together.

Well, I just got to hold her.
I touched her perfect head
and I'll tell you this:

My sister is whole.

SEVEN

Interview with Janet S. Wong

Janet S. Wong has written several fine collections of poetry as well as a number of picture books. Janet's poems are inventive and human. They have a way of somehow bringing me deeper into my own life. Janet's books include Good Luck Gold; A Suitcase of Seaweed; The Rainbow Hand: Poems about Mothers and Children; Behind the Wheel: Poems about Driving; *and* Night Garden: Poems from the World of Dreams. *She lives in Seattle, Washington.*

Why do you write poetry? I mean, what's in it for you?

I love writing poems because I love playing with words—but I hate doing it for long stretches of time. It takes only five minutes to write a good draft of a poem. I can jot down a first draft of a poem and then go and eat a bag of potato chips; come back and spend five minutes writing a second, different draft and go for a swim; write a third draft the next day or the next week, and so on. With poems, revision is fun, too—and easier than with some other forms of writing. Big changes can come about from changing a free verse draft into a rhyming draft, a long draft into a haiku, a poem with hodgepodge rhythm into one with definite and regular beats. I write between ten and fifty drafts of most of my poems, and the hardest part is always having to choose the draft—or parts of drafts—I like best. What's in it for me? The terrific feeling that comes when I read something I love—and can say, "I wrote that!"

What other published poets have influenced your work?

Myra Cohn Livingston was my teacher and mentor. She sold my first book, *Good Luck Gold*, for me. She also was the person who transformed me from a poetry hater into a poetry lover. Around fourth grade I started hating poetry—at least I hated the poems I knew, which mainly were poems by dead English poets, poems I didn't understand very well. When I heard Myra read her poem "There Was a Place" (from the book of the same title), I started thinking differently about poems.

How has your ethnic background influenced your poetry?

Some of my best poems are Asian-themed, I think, since they focus very closely on memories of real-life experiences that I have had with my family—and we happen to be Asian. But most of my poems come from my everyday life, which happens to be here in urban/suburban America—so I'd like to think that people of any ethnic background can find meaning in them.

Your poems seem to be little stories. But in your picture book, Buzz, *you play with the sounds of words. When you write a poem, do you attend mostly to meaning, or to sound? Or both?*

I usually concentrate on meaning when I write a poem or picture-book story, but sometimes I will use sound to help get my idea across. I just finished writing a long poem for a picture book called *Hooray for You, Swimmer.* It doesn't contain a regular rhyme, but does have a fair amount of internal rhyme—rhyme sounds buried in the middle of lines, used somewhat randomly. Somewhere around my fortieth draft I decided I wanted the reader to speed through a certain section of it, and so I changed some of the meaning to allow myself to create a whole section full of easy rhymes that—I hope—will sweep the reader up as if he were riding a wave of sound.

What are your thoughts about writing in different poetic forms?

Almost everything I know about poetry I learned from Myra Cohn Livingston, and the first thing she taught was form. She believed very firmly that "you need to learn the rules before you can break them," and she gave us exercises to do: couplets, tercets, and quatrains; haiku and limericks and sonnets; and even more unusual forms such as the *villanelle* and the *triolet*. I worked hard on the exercises and learned them—and then I forgot them.

Now I never write limericks or sonnets or villanelles or triolets; I write almost always in free verse or in one of the three basic rhyme forms: couplets, tercets, and quatrains. But the training in forms taught me to be sensitive to the word games poets can play, to pay greater attention to what is going on in a poem during my readings of it—either a poem of my own or someone else's. I am sure my work is much richer because of this sensitivity.

When do you write? Do you stick to a regular schedule?

I write whenever I can fit it in. Five minutes, as I said earlier, is not too short a time to get a draft—or even a part of a draft—down on paper.

Do you ever run into writer's block?

I am very good at getting words down on paper (especially in the computer). They're not always the "right" words, but the most important part of writing, I think, is the beginning: getting words—any words—written. I think E-mail has helped me in this, since I answer dozens of messages daily. Practice keeps my writing muscles in order, even if I'm just writing short notes to my friends! I used to have a horrible procrastination problem because I was often afraid that the thing I'd write wouldn't be good enough. That was before I worked revision into my writing routine. Now I rarely have trouble with writing a draft, since I know it won't be my only draft!

Do you have any advice for young writers?

Read, read, read! This is what Myra Cohn Livingston told me when I started studying poetry with her. The more you read, the better a writer you'll be.

EIGHT

Wordplay

One, two! One, two! And through and through
The vorpal blade went snicker-snack!
> —LEWIS CARROLL
> FROM *"Jabberwocky"*

One morning my sons Robert and Joseph were eating cereal.

"It's Manager's Special today for school lunch," I told them as I read the school lunch calendar. "Do you want to buy that?"

"That sounds terrible," Robert (fifth grade) moaned.

"Think positive," I said. "It could be something delicious."

"It's a risk!" Joseph (first grade) put in.

"Yeah," Robert said. "They should call it Manager's Risk."

Some people speak in a way that's downright clever. Their talk is peppered by humor, wit, puns, sarcasm—and that makes them interesting to listen to. You can do the same thing with a poem, playing with words in a way that will make the reader sit up and take notice.

Lots of poems come out—well—flat. Ordinary. A good poem often needs at least a little surprise to help it come alive, to lift it off the page and into the reader's imagination. In the following poem, Katelyn and Jenny Walter have chosen a topic (sunset) that has been written about by many poets. But their wordplay keeps the poem fresh and lively:

Sun set

sun set
fun set
to see what
you could see;
birds flying

everywhere except
far underneath me.
Fly away, fly away,
into the sun set.
Fly away, fly away,
into the fun set.

J. Patrick Lewis is one of the masters of word-play. Look at this short poem of his:

Robin

Suddenly Spring wings
into the backyard, ready
to play tug-of-worm.

Here the poet describes an ordinary moment in an ordinary way until that little word twist at the end. We expect him to say "to play tug-of-war," but he puts the whammy on us and substitutes *worm* for *war*. Tug-of-worm is an invention we've never heard of, yet when Lewis writes it we delight in his cleverness and get a clear image at the same time.

When I was a little boy, I was fascinated by words

that sounded the same when you said them out loud, but might be spelled differently and might mean two or even three things: *bare* and *bear*; *C, see,* and *sea*; etc. Those words are called *homonyms,* though of course I didn't know that at the time. That sort of wordplay comes in very handy to a writer.

I love to play with different meanings of the same word. Often I try to incorporate a double meaning into a poem. Consider these four lines from my book *Twilight Comes Twice*:

Dawn slowly brightens
the empty baseball field,
polishing the diamond
until it shines.

A double meaning adds depth and resonance to a poem. "Polishing the diamond" is a pun—something that means two things at the same time. Puns like this serve notice to your reader: Stay awake! Pay attention! Not only that, but they can be fun to write. I found a hilarious example of this in a book titled *Walking on the Bridge of Your Nose: Wordplay, Poems, and Rhymes,* edited by

Michael Rosen. Here's the anonymous poem:

> Do you carrot all for me?
> My heart beets for you,
> With your turnip nose
> And your radish face.
> You are a peach.
> If we cantaloupe,
> Lettuce marry;
> Weed make a swell pear.

Some words have their own sound effects built into them. Words like *buzzing* bees, a *clap* of thunder, *hiss*, *pop*, and *murmur* all make the sound that they are describing. Words like this contain their own kind of music. The word for this is *onomatopoeia*, and if you can spell it without looking at it you're a far better speller than I am. Edgar Allan Poe used this technique while penning a famous poem that included the lines

> To the tintinnabulation that so musically wells
> From the bells, bells, bells, bells,
>   Bells, bells, bells—

Tintinnabulation is a musical word that makes me hear high, metallic bell sounds. But onomatopoeia isn't some kind of fancy idea only famous poets can use. Ross Wells, a sixth grader, used this technique while writing a poem about a leaky faucet at his grandmother's house:

At Grandma's House

In that ancient bathtub,
The drip, drop,
Dripping, dropping,
Drip-drip-dripping,
Dinking, plinking,
Never-stopping,
Tor-tor-torturing,
Of that faucet
Assassinated
Any chance I had to
Sleep!

When I write poems, I also enjoy using words that don't exactly say their own sounds but are flat-out fun to say. In my newest book of poetry,

Have You Been to the Beach Lately?, I used lots of wordplay in poems like this one:

The First Time

On my first trip to the beach
the sea refused to cooperate.

It kept curling and whirling
    bobbing and weaving
    clearing its throat
    whenever a wave drew back.

It kept moving and grooving
    shucking and jiving
    dishing and dancing
    razzling and dazzling

wouldn't keep still even
long enough to shake hands.

Play with words. Go wild! Have fun! If you're having fun, there's a good chance your readers will, too.

NINE

Troubleshooting

Every poem is an infant labored into birth. . . .
—JIMMY SANTIAGO BACA

Sometimes you hear a writer tell about a poem that just "wrote itself." Believe me: That is rare. Most of my poems don't just materialize out of thin air. And most of the time they don't come out right, at least not the first time around. I have to rejigger, rework, start over. As you remember from Chapter 7, Janet S. Wong usually writes ten to fifty drafts of a poem. The same thing may happen to you. There are many different ways that a poem can go wrong. In this chapter we'll look at some most common problems you may run into while trying to write a poem. Then I'll offer some suggestions for what you can do about them.

The rhyme doesn't sound right. In one fourth-grade class I met a girl who wrote a poem that began like this:

> On Valentine's Day you get presents
> And sometimes you get nesents.

"What's a nesent?" I asked.

"Well, it's just a silly word I invented to rhyme with present," she admitted with a sheepish smile.

Rhyming is great. When I was very little I memorized nursery rhymes, just like many other kids. In elementary school many students fall in love with rhyming poems by Jack Prelusky and Shel Silverstein. Those poets make rhyming look easy. Their rhyming poems are fun to read, say out loud, memorize.

But it can be harder when you try to write your own rhymes. How many words can you think of that rhyme with orange? How many words rhyme with wreath? I have seen hundreds of poems—and written dozens myself!—where you can tell that a certain word was used only because it rhymed with another word.

"Sometimes you try to use rhyme in a poem," poet Georgia Heard says, "but what happens instead is that rhyme ends up using you!"

If you're having trouble rhyming your poem, consider changing it to a free verse form. This doesn't always work, but I've found that some poems do sound better when written in free verse. Free verse poems can sound more natural because they resemble human conversation. Plus you're not straightjacketed into a particular rhyme scheme. If you want to get a feel for free verse poetry, check the back of this book, where I have provided a list of good free verse poetry books. And reread the section on line breaks in Chapter 6.

Still not willing to give up on rhyme? Fine. You'll need to get in the habit of rereading your poem several times. Rereading is crucial: You need to be an expert on your poem, and know it from top to bottom, inside and out. Reread with both your eyes and your ears. Say it aloud. Does it look right? Does it sound right?

When you're trying to untangle a snarl of yarn or string, it doesn't work too well if you pull the string tight. It works better if you keep the tangled string loose as you look for ways to untie the knots. The same thing is true when you're trying to use rhyme in a poem. I find it helpful to keep the rhyme loose, and not get too committed to any one word, until the poem sounds exactly the way I want it to sound.

It's a story, not a poem. This is a common problem. Human beings are natural storytellers, so it's not surprising when a poem morphs into a story right before our eyes. In Chapter 6 we talked about how to create line breaks in a poem, but that's not enough. When you take a story and use line breaks to break up the sentences, the result is *not* a poem, as you can see from this example of my own writing:

> On Christmas morning
> I saw a bright blue package
> with little holes in the top
> and when I opened it a little brown

nose poked out. My puppy!
So cute! I played with him all
day and took him out for a walk
on a leash and fed him his first
dish of chow. He fell asleep on my
lap when I was watching the
football game and when he woke
up he pulled the tablecloth off the
dining-room table and caused a huge
spill.

These sentences have been divided up to make it look like a poem, but it's really a story. This piece about the new puppy is like a video—a series of images. In contrast, it may help to think of a poem as a snapshot. (There are some exceptions for longer poems, such as epics and ballads.) A snapshot has one image. If your poem sounds like a story, it may be because you have crammed too many images into it.

What to do? Focus. Pick out one image, one moment, and concentrate on writing about that. The piece about the puppy might have worked better if I'd tried to capture the moment when I saw the puppy for the first time. Or the first time the puppy fell asleep at the foot of my bed.

Here's another idea: Reread your draft and underline those parts that sound most like a poem. Copy only those lines onto a separate sheet of paper and start with them. See if you can write some new lines that fit with the ones from the original draft. The new lines should take the reader deeper into the moment you're trying to create. Think snapshot, not video.

My poem has a wicked case of the blahs. Some poems don't make you sit up in your seat. In fact, they make you yawn! This can happen for lots of reasons. Often poets pick topics that are too general: rainbows, flowers, baseball . . .

If your poem feels dull, narrow your focus by taking a slice of your general topic. For example, instead of writing about roses in general, try writing about those damaged roses that never get sent to lovers. Instead of writing about baseball, you could write about the infield dirt, perfect and unblemished, the instant before the first fielder steps onto it. Think small.

Warning: Beware list poems! Many kids love to

write them, but they are hard to pull off. When you write about *green* by listing all the green things in the world, it's hard to make the poem tight. The more specific and personal you can make your poem, the better it will be.

Your poem may have the blahs because the language is flat. I often find that a poem needs a little twist, a stretch, an unusual phrase, something that lifts it off the ground. The first part of my poem "Great Blue Heron" begins with a straightforward description:

> Even when we walk up close
> he pays no attention to us
> as he walks along the shore
> peering into shallow water
> looking for some juicy crab
> or unsuspecting sushi.
>
> He looks like a dorky teacher
> teaching advanced algebra,
> all eyes and bones and beak,
> lecturing to invisible students,
> hungry for that one moment

when he will get across his
                              point.

I knew if I simply described this bird I would
risk losing the reader. That's why I incorporated a
little surprise in the sixth line. The words *unsus-*
pecting sushi contain lots of *S* sounds. *Sushi* makes
a rhyme with *juicy* from the preceding line. But
mainly I thought it was funny to apply the fancy
word "sushi" to a blue heron's fresh-killed supper.

One more thing, and this may be the most
important of all: Your poem may be dull because
there is no voice. By *no voice* I mean that it sounds
nothing like you. Instead it sounds like something
anybody could have written. Reread your poem
and ask yourself: Where am I in the poem? You
don't actually have to use *I*, but you should be
able to recognize some part of the way you say
things, or how you see the world:

The Petroglyph

A petroglyph,
Lines carved out of solid stone.

The hours and hours
It must have taken to carve you.
How old you must be.
Hundreds maybe thousands of years old
Being repaved with land
By the new lava flows.
I would like to meet the one who
Carved you out of the stone
With those ancient tools so long ago.

Jeremy Lota, this poem's author, is a middle-school student in Hawaii. His poem is about a carving on a rock, and it could have been stone-cold boring, except that you can hear Jeremy's voice. He makes his voice come alive by speaking to the rocks, and by bringing himself in at the very end.

My poem is too vague and "floaty." I met one junior-high student who showed me this poem he had written:

Spiraling into depths uncharted,
arrows of deceit shower.
The appointed one labors
under burdens of unceasing pain.

Cures lie in the chosen soul,
whose touch enervates
to unforeseen vistas.
Matters not the vision to be achieved.
Reality possesses truth
and does not renounce the future.

I don't understand this poem. In fact, when I read it I feel as if I'm drowning in too many complicated, highfalutin, four-syllable words. True, the vocabulary is impressive, but the meaning of this poem is hidden. A poem must be more than just a bunch of pretty words. A poem should be *about* something. I'm not sure what this is about. Maybe this writer knew what he wanted to say, but the words and images he chose didn't get across his idea, at least not to me.

Antennas often need to be grounded so the electrical charge does not burn up the TV or radio. In the same way, it's helpful to "ground" the big ideas in your poem by using things that are—well—more down to earth. Natural objects (rocks, shells, clouds) that are concrete and specific give the reader something real and tangible to relate to. The following poem of my own is about losing connection with another person, but I try to ground the ideas in the physical things of this world:

The Sweater

You give back my sweater,
the maroon one you wore
the last time I saw you.

I wash it by hand and pin it
taut on the clothesline
before I leave for the day.

I come home in heavy rain,
the sweater too soaked
to try to bring inside.

Rain and more rain. What cycles
will it go through
while I sleep in my bed:

bleaches of moonlight,
rinses of darkness and wind?
Will the sweater ever be dry?

And dried stiff
by the sweet fall sun
will it ever again feel like mine?

The poem goes on too long. There are a couple of reasons why this happens. As you get older you often have more to say about a particular topic. And you can sustain longer and longer pieces of writing. As a result your poems get longer.

But there may be another reason. It may be that you don't trust the reader. Some poems present an image, then remind the reader of the image, and then explain what the image means. You may be surprised to find out that the reader understood what you were getting at all along. A poem should capture a moment, not try to explain it. The poet Robert Morgan says: "I like poems in fragments, things with rough and sharp edges, that sometimes cut unexpectedly, that cannot be handled too easily. . . . Lines are pieces of the shattered original diamond."

Remember: A poem is a sprint, not a marathon. Beware of going on and on and draining the energy out of your poem. When you have written the last image, stop. Your poem is finished.

TEN

Interview with J. Patrick Lewis

J. Patrick Lewis is a clever, funny, endlessly inventive poet. His books include Freedom Like Sunlight: Praise-songs for Black Americans; The Bookworm's Feast; At the Wish of the Fish; *and* Isabella Abnormella and the Very, Very Finicky Queen of Trouble. *Lewis's poetry is very entertaining, but you can also learn a lot about writing by reading his work. He is a careful crafts-man with words. He has a way of making his kind of writing look easy. Which it isn't.*

Why do you write poetry?

When I consider the alternatives to writing poetry, none of them appeals to me, not even remotely. Poetry, I have said elsewhere, is ear candy. It's a blind date with enchantment. It's the first refuge against indifference. Reading poems—and you should always read them out loud, even when you are reading alone—can change your life. As the poet Mary Oliver has written, poems are "fires for the cold, ropes let down to the lost, something as necessary as bread in the pockets of the hungry." So who wouldn't want to be intimately involved in such a grand purpose?

What other published poets have influenced your work?

Not long ago a young woman, who wanted very much to write children's poetry, asked me for some advice. "Which poets do you enjoy reading?" I asked encouragingly. "Good heavens," she said, "I never read poetry. After all, I wouldn't want to be affected by what others have written." What I remember saying in response is that, quite apart from the sheer thrill of reading, another poet's words or lines might be the catalyst to her own magnum opus. And after all, would she ever consider becoming a pianist or a painter without studying very carefully the works of others?

But the short answer to your question is: All of them. Every time you read a poem, the good and the great anyway, you can't help but be affected, even if that influence is very small and unidentifiable. The adult poets whose work touches me comprise an endless list. The great poets for children I return to again and again are Edward Lear and Lewis Carroll. Many fine children's poets are writing today, but I wouldn't want to begin naming them for fear of leaving someone out.

Where do you get your ideas?

Three places: From reading, observing, and remembering the events of my life and my children's lives.

Could you give us the origin/genesis of a particular poem?

I'm a library groupie, so I am always eager to sing its praises. My latest collection to be accepted for publication, *Please Bury Me in the Library: Poems About Books and Reading,* is a homage to every house of books. One day I was thinking about just how pleasant it would be to find one's final resting place in the proximity of good books. Here's what came of it—the title poem from the collection.

Please Bury Me in the Library

Please bury me in the library
In the clean, well-lighted stacks
Of Novels, History, Poetry
Right next to the Paperbacks,

Where the Kids' Books dance
With True Romance
And the Dictionary dozes.
Please bury me in the library
With a dozen long-stemmed proses

Way back by a rack of Magazines.
I won't be sad too often
If they bury me in the library
With Bookworms in my coffin.

What sorts of prewriting/brainstorming (notebook, sketchbook, journal, walking, etc.) do you find helpful?

Communing with nature, keeping a journal, joining writers' workshops—all of these undoubtedly inspire the aspiring. I confess I don't do any of them. My twin brother, who is my alter ego, and I talk quite a bit about books, reading, and writing. He is the first to receive whatever I have written, and I trust his judgment implicitly. My one concession to brainstorming is that I keep a daybook of lines/sentences/thoughts discovered in wondrous places. Here's a modest example: "I wonder how all those who do not write, compose, or paint can manage to escape the madness, the melancholia, the panic fear which is inherent in the human situation." (Graham Greene)

Many writers find it hard to begin writing. Do you? How do you start?

I wish I could say the Muse whispers to me each morning as soon as I'm comfortably seated. Alas. I suspect she is still sleeping. Poems can begin with a single word or phrase, or from a mental picture. But most often I try to begin by thinking about an entire collection of poems— about sports, holidays, riddles, geography, and so forth. I do research or I read other poems on the same subject to help me wrap my mind around it. Recently, for example, I decided to write a group of math poems, which I've called *Arithmetickle Me!* When I had written and rewritten (over several months!) forty or so math poems that I thought were worthy, I sent them to my editor.

When do you write? Do you stick to a regular schedule?

When I am not making school visits or attending conferences, you can find me each morning at 7 A.M. in front of my computer. From then until about 5 P.M., I will be writing, rewriting, reading, occasionally corresponding with friends and editors. It's a routine I rarely vary, even on weekends.

Do you ever run into writer's block?

After finishing a project, a manuscript, I invariably succumb to a bout of the blues. It may last for several weeks . . . until the next idea comes along, and I'm off and running again. When writer's block rears its ugly head, I turn to writing letters instead—or switch gears entirely and turn to another poetry subject. Or, best of all, I read fiction or poetry on the back porch with a good cup of coffee and goldfinch gossip.

What sorts of revisions do you typically do?

I do scores of revisions on every poem. Which may mean chucking out an entire stanza or even a whole poem, or it may mean tinkering with individual words. Since verbs are the muscles of good writing (and adjectives are the fat), I will spend hours trying to uncover that elusive verb or metaphor that one hopes will make a reader stop, ever so briefly, in wonder. Needless to say, that is the most difficult—and rewarding—part of rewriting.

Is your editor an important part of your process?

Editors, gifted as many of them are, generally have a greater impact on my prose than on my verse. They will blue-pencil a story manuscript more often than a poetry manuscript. And editors talk funny. If a poem doesn't tickle an editor's fancy, she may say, "I don't love it," which is editorialese for, "I wouldn't publish this poem on the no-sir side of a mule!" In which case, I will take it out of the collection altogether.

Do you have any advice for young writers?

Never write more than you read—that message comes to you from the brilliant Dr. Samuel Johnson of over 200 years ago.

As the late poet John Ciardi once told me, Get yourself a big wastebasket, and keep it filled. Most words writers write aren't worth the trees that are cut down to publish them. If you want to be a writer, you must first agree to be a rewriter.

Find your own voice. Try not to write like anyone else but yourself. Salvador Dalí once remarked that the first person to compare the cheeks of a girl to a rose was obviously a poet; the first to repeat it was possibly an idiot.

Unanchor your imagination. No subject is out of bounds for poetry.

Resist the temptation to rhyme. That may seem odd coming from me. I consider sound every bit as important as sense, and I believe young children being introduced to poetry or verse connect immediately with its music. But—a very big "but"—rhyming is not one of your holiday games. Like painting or learning to play the piano, writing poetry takes a slow hand. For writers of rhyme, the bar of excellence is raised a notch or two because contrived, hackneyed rhymes are so easy to write—and so painful to read. A child coming to writing invariably chooses the easy rhyme that's completely forced. The results are woeful.

Instead, do what you do best, which is to revel in surprising, sometimes wholly original metaphors and similes that are the envy of all poets. You have a knack for "saying the darnedest things"—until, like all of us adults, you lose that natural ability at about the age of 11 or so.

Finally, the novelist Allan Gurganus has recently said, in another context, "In America, the true 'F' word is *failure*." When I make school visits I emphasize how important it is to fail—regularly. What comes easy is cheesy. So embrace failure. It can be your best and most honest friend. Failure is the surest road to success.

ELEVEN

A Few Words About Form

Why do we value form? Perhaps the answer lies in the secrets of our musculature, in our dark roots. Why do we live in square rooms? Why do we draw mechanical doodles when we are bored? Why do we tap our feet to music? Perhaps there is a profound link between the meter of verse and the human pulse, the rhythm of life itself.
—ROBERT WALLACE

Poetry comes in countless forms—haiku, free verse, limericks, odes, sonnets, acrostic poems, cinquains, couplets, diamantes, etc. So many forms can make you a little dizzy. Some, like acrostics and diamantes, are recent inventions that are found mostly in schools, while a form like haiku goes back thousands of years.

This book focuses more on the "inside" of poetry (ideas, images, feelings) than on the "outside" (appearance, form). For this reason I have decided not to delve deeply into poetic forms. I think it's important, however, that we spend some time exploring this topic. I have met many students who enjoy the challenge of trying to write in a particular form.

"For me it's easier than free verse," one girl explained to me, "because I already have the pattern I'm supposed to follow."

Other writers feel constricted when asked to shoehorn their words and ideas into a particular poetic form.

"It feels like I'm in a straitjacket!" one boy told me. "I mean, I feel like I can't breathe!"

I know what he means. But I have also found that the opposite can happen. It sounds like a paradox but it's true: Sometimes being forced to write in a particular form liberates my mind and prompts me to write a poem that is bold, new, original.

Has this ever happened to you? You try a sport for the very first time and it feels strange, clumsy. Then you figure it out and . . . you're pretty good! Your friends say: "Whoa! This guy's a natural!" The different forms of poetry are like different kinds of sports—each has its own rules, traditions, skills, challenges. You might try one and be surprised to discover that you're actually better at it than you could have imagined. Let's take a look at a few poetic forms—what they are, what makes them tick, how you can write them yourself.

Haiku. A few years ago I began experimenting with haiku. A friend had given me a book of Japanese haiku, and as I read it I was struck by how simple it seemed. Three lines, a few words: haiku! I had learned in school that the first line of haiku has five syllables, the second has seven, and the third has five. But this book made me want to go deeper, to discover what haiku was about. I read some books and learned that haiku is like a discipline. I learned that the five-seven-five rhythm of the three lines is meant to reflect the rhythm of the human breath. I also discovered that haiku

- is attentive to space and time—often the season of the year.
- uses plain language.
- demands accurate and original images drawn from everyday life.
- communicates a little revelation: Aha!

If you look closely at J. Patrick Lewis's poem "Robin" on page 82, you'll discover that it is actually a haiku. Reading and learning about haiku inspired me to try to write one of my own:

in early morning
a swarm of silver minnows
rush hour round my feet

The challenge of haiku lies in creating a visual poem with a just a few words. The following haiku were written by junior-high students in New York City:

haiku by Liang Zhuo Qi

Lonely piece of dust,
hiding in a dim corner,
waiting for the broom.

haiku by Jia Cheng Mei

The sky is too huge,
daytime it is a river,
nighttime it is ink.

Ode. Some years ago I was in a first-grade class. There I met a little boy who was enthusiastically writing poems, one after another, and each one had a title that went like this:

O to the Sun
O to My Mom

I was a bit confused until I realized that he was trying to write an *ode*! The dictionary tells us that an ode is a lyric poem, rhymed or unrhymed, in which the poet speaks to some person or thing. An ode is characterized by lofty emotion. To put it more simply, you write an ode to praise something you admire. Romantic poets like John Keats wrote odes to the people and things that inspired them. But when you write an ode, you don't have to choose a big topic like God or country. You might have some fun writing an ode to a more mundane subject. Here's a poem by Becky Gallagher, a student in Princeton, New Jersey. You'll notice that in her ode, Becky doesn't write *about* shampoo, she actually speaks *to* it:

O Shampoo!

As you tangle through my wet hair,
your lemony extract fills the
steamy air.
How you mush and squush!
Cunningly, you pick your way through
the steaming rain.
O Shampoo!
What strategic stuff has Paul Mitchell

put in your
ivory plastic casing?
Shampoo,
A companion to trust,
I can decisively dedicate my shower time to
This gel from the heavens!

Finally, your concentrated
beautifier
is washed away with the massaging steady
rainstorm

Leaving
my
hair
proud.

Free verse. Are there any rules in your school that seem strict or unfair? That's the way it was in the world of poetry. For many centuries, poems had to follow prescribed rules. Some poets didn't like all those rules. They found them restrictive. Poets like Walt Whitman, e.e. cummings, Marianne

Moore, and William Carlos Williams rebelled against those traditional forms and wrote in free verse. I use free verse for most of my poems. Robert Frost wrote some free verse poems, though he once compared free verse to playing tennis without a net—too easy, no fun. If you're interested in using free verse for your poetry, you'll want to carefully reread the section on line breaks in Chapter 6.

Found poetry. Imagine what would happen if you were to dig in the sand at the beach and find a chunk of gold. True, you didn't make that gold, but if you find it, it's yours.

The same thing can happen with poetry. Occasionally, you will find words that capture your attention. One time while I was visiting Northampton, Massachusetts, I saw a man on the street with a pile of pamphlets. The man kept chanting: "Buy my poetry! Buy my poetry! Fifty cents a copy! If you won't buy it, I can't sell it! Don't make me work at McDonald's!" I really felt for this guy, but the things he said made me laugh, too. When I wrote his words in my notebook, they made a poem:

Buy My Poetry!

Buy my poetry!
50 cents a copy!
If you won't buy it,
I can't sell it!
Don't make me work at
McDonald's!

The words that capture your attention could be spoken. They could be printed somewhere, on a subway or magazine ad, for example. Write them down, and arrange them to look like a poem.

Concrete poetry. While this is not exactly a form, it is a particular kind of poem in which the poet arranges the words on the page to reflect the meaning. For example, in my poem "Water Seeks Its Own Level," the narrator's sister takes a shower and doesn't notice that her feet are covering the drain. This creates a terrible flood. Here's how the poem ends:

and makes a small lake that spills out

onto the front steps and t

          r

           i

            c

             k

              l

               e

                s

down to the rose bushes
she has forgotten to
water

Are you writing about snow? You could write your poem in such a way that words are falling through the air. Writing a poem about a tornado? See what happens when you arrange the words on the page so that they twist back on themselves. Experiment. Poetry gives you the freedom to place words on the page in any way or shape you want. This gives you a way to visually reinforce what your poem is about.

Imitation. Lots of students feel that they are not supposed to imitate other poets' work—ever!

Imitation sounds too much like copying, which sounds like plagiarism, which sounds like stealing, which sounds like . . . expulsion! (Which sounds like prison!)

Slow down. If you read a four-line poem about a cat, there's no law that says you can't write your own four-line poem about cats. Poets borrow things like line lengths, rhythms, cool words from each other all the time. Go for it!

As you read poetry, you'll find that many poems follow a particular format or pattern. It can be fun trying to imitate a format or pattern you find in another poem. My friend Suzanne Gardinier, a poet and teacher, calls this "putting on the poem's shirt." She reminds her college students that it's okay to wear this shirt, to get inspired by the original poem, while you're writing your own. Take my poem "Bedtime":

Sometimes I remember
the good old days

sitting on the kitchen floor
at night with my brother

each on our own squares
of cool linoleum.

I'm fresh from the bath,
wearing baseball pajamas.

Outside the screen door
summer breezes stir.

Mom gives us each two cookies,
a cup of milk, a kiss goodnight.

I still can't imagine
anything better than that.

I invite you to "put on this poem's shirt" and
try writing your own poem based on the format I
used. Start with the same first stanza, and end with
the same stanza I use to end my poem. In the
middle, go back and describe a particular
memory from when you were little. You decide
whether or not you want to use two-line stanzas, as
I did.

Invention. You don't have to limit yourself to a

form somebody has cooked up for you. See if you can come up with your own. As I write a poem, I often try to invent my own form or pattern that feels right for what I'm trying to say. Then I follow that form throughout the whole poem.

For example, I wrote a poem called "How to Make a Snow Angel." The poem begins with a person making footsteps through the snow. I decided to use short, two-line stanzas. This would make the poem look like a little like footprints. Plus there would be lots of white space in the poem. Here it is:

How to Make a Snow Angel

Go alone or with a best friend.
Find a patch of unbroken snow.

Walk on tiptoes. Step backwards
Into your very last footprints.

Slowly sit back onto the snow.
Absolutely do not use your hands.

By now you should by lying flat
With snow fitting snug around you.

Let your eyes drink some blue sky.
Close them. Breathe normally.

Move your arms back and forth.
Concentrate. Think: snow angel.

In a minute don't be surprised
If you start feeling a little funny.

Big and small. Warm and cold.
Your breath light as a snowflake.

Sweep your legs back and forth
But keep both eyes tightly closed.

Keep moving the arms until they
Lift, tremble, wobble or float.

Stand without using your hands.
Take time to get your balance.

Take three deep breaths.
Open your eyes.

Stretch. Float. Fly!

Trying out a particular form might open up unexpected things in your writing. But at other times the form might feel forced, awkward, and you will know it's not right. It's not you. That's okay. I encourage you to experiment with different forms, but don't ever feel locked into any one of them.

Form should be an invitation to a writer, not a straitjacket. I hope you'll try to look at form as possibility instead of punishment. I feel about form the way I feel about rhyme—it's great, but in too many classrooms it has been overdone. Overcooked. I like mine barbequed medium-rare. Juicy.

TWELVE

Going Public

Every poem is a blow against silence.
—Carlos Fuentes

Okay, so you've written a poem, maybe lots of them. Now what? Writing the poem is hugely important, but your job is only half done. The next step involves deciding how (or whether) to send your poem out into the world. In this chapter, I'm going to suggest several ways to go public with what you have written.

Make a collection of your poems. A poetry collection feels like a book. If you have enough pages, you might think about making copies for friends and family.

Begin by studying collections of poems by other poets. Most poem collections are organized around a particular theme: love, family, endangered animals, baseball, etc. (Kristine O'Connell George's book *Toasting Marshmallows*, for example, is a collection of camping poems.) Ask yourself if you want your collection to revolve around one subject. On the other hand, you may prefer to put together a collection of your favorite poems on a variety of subjects.

Think about how you want to organize your collection. I've learned that separate sections can be helpful to the reader. In my book *I Am Wings: Poems About Love*, I found there were lots of romantic poems but also many poems about jealousy, breaking up, etc. I decided to title one section Falling In and the other Falling Out. The poems I had written "fell" naturally into one section or the other.

Think about the title. Let's say you have written fifteen poems about porpoises. Instead of a simple label like *Porpoise Poems*, consider a more intriguing title like *Sensational Singers of the Sea*. If you did that you could use *Porpoise Poems* as a sub-title. You will also want a table of contents so your reader can find particular poems. Finally, think about the illustrations. Beware of overwhelming your readers with dazzling neon-colored paintings. Many poetry collections include pencil sketches or black-and-white illustrations. The idea is to give just enough of an illustration so that each reader can still make a personal image from your poem.

BYOP Party: Bring Your Own Poem. It sounds sort of funny, but my friends and I had just such a party for ten years in a row. We held the party around Christmastime, when people seem to appreciate taking a few hours from the hectic holiday season to consider the important things in life. With its emphasis on both celebration and reflection, poetry was the perfect centerpiece for our party.

A BYOP party is easy. All you need is some people and a place to hold it. Food, drink, and music are good, too. When you invite people, you can ask them to bring a poem to read aloud. They can either bring a poem they have written themselves, or a favorite poem that they have read.

You'll want to organize the poetry reading so that nobody gets left out. I'd suggest making a list of who is going to read. If you have lots of readers (a nice problem!) take a refreshment break halfway through. Try hard to limit readers to no more than five minutes. Trust me: Nothing kills the spirit quicker than a person who gets up with thirty pages of deadly poetry and insists on reading every page.

The spirit of a BYOP party should be celebratory rather than competitive. Lots of applause after certain readers have finished or certain poems have been read can build a sense of competition. At our BYOP parties we ask the audience to hold applause until all readers have finished.

Read it aloud. Here we are near the end of this book, but reading aloud is so important I probably should have written about it on page one! Like flame to paper, something ignites when a human voice lifts written poetry into the realm of sound. More than any other kind of writing (except maybe a play), poetry is meant to be read aloud.

At a BYOP party, *how* you read a poem will be almost as important as the poem itself. Reading aloud is a skill separate from writing the poem. My friend Lisa Bianchi talks about three stages to reading aloud:

Stage One: reading the poem for the first time. Your first reading of a poem will probably be awkward, halting, not very good. But that's okay. Actresses and actors consider a Stage One reading of a script to be very important. The first time around, your mouth and voice will meet the poem for the first time. You're just trying to get comfortable.

Stage Two: Becoming comfortable with the poem. When you move to a new town, it's hard to know how to get from one place to another. But after a few tries (and a few times getting lost) your feet start to know where to go. In the same way, you begin to know a poem after you have read it four, five, six times. You know what to expect, so you don't tend to stumble over particular words.

Stage Three: knowing it cold. In his song "Hard Rain" Bob Dylan says: "I'll know my song well before I start singing." If you keep practicing, reading a poem aloud over and over, you can get to that point, too. Now you barely have to look at the page. Since you no longer stumble over words, you can relax, look at your audience, and put expression into the words you are reading. It's a wonderful feeling when you know a poem so well it has truly become part of you.

Choral reading. This is a great way to spice up a BYOP party. In a choral reading, a small group of people stand up to read and interpret a poem. Here are some guidelines for preparing for the choral reading ahead of time:

1) Get into groups of four. The energy peters out with two people, and groups of six can be unwieldy. I have found from experience that four is about right.

2) Figure out which poem you're going to present. Make sure that each person has a copy of the poem.

3) Read it through silently.

4) Read it aloud together.

5) Which lines seem to be important? Mark them.

6) Read it aloud again and decide who will read which lines. Are there certain lines you want to read together? Or would it be more effective if only one person reads a line? A group of lines?

7) Are there places where your voice changes—gets louder, sadder, angrier?

8) Do you want to include physical movement as a way to enhance the meaning of the poem? This is your chance to go wild and ham it up, if appropriate to the poem.

9) Read it again, incorporating any final changes.

10) Have a blast!

There are many other, less splashy ways of going public with your poem:

Send it to someone special. After you visit your grandmother in Florida, you get on a plane and write a poem about her. Great. Copy it onto a nice piece of paper, put it into an envelope, and send it off to her. She will treasure it forever.

Of course, some poems are simply too personal, too private, too raw to share with anyone.

In that case:

Copy it into your writer's notebook. I think of my notebook as an extra chamber of my heart—a place where I can feel perfectly comfortable stashing a special poem or other tidbit from my inner life.

Put a poem in your pocket or wallet. I have two very personal poems written for me by special people in my life. I would die if just anyone read those poems, so I keep them tucked in a compartment of my wallet where I can take them out when I want to reread them.

Memorize it. You can do this with one of your own poems or a poem someone else has written for you. This isn't the same as publishing your poem in a magazine, but it is a way to let your poem live forever inside of you. Think about it: when we have memorized a poem, we say we "know it by heart." In other words, it has become a part of our deepest self.

My brother Tom has written a book of poems titled *Falling Through the Earth.* The book is eighty-eight pages long, and he has memorized every poem in it!

"Once I had memorized my poems, I found myself saying them in my head, or while I was driving, or just sitting by myself," Tom says. "It sounds funny, but I have gotten so much pleasure from my own poems."

Some Recommended
Poetry Books

Here are some of my favorite poetry collections. In these books you'll find plenty of poems you can apprentice yourself to. This list is meant to go beyond the poets (Whitman, Tennyson, etc.) that students typically read in school.

Angelou, Maya. *Life Doesn't Frighten Me*. Stewart, Tabori & Chang, 1988. Book is one long poem about courage.

Clifton, Lucille. *Some of the Days of Everett Anderson*. Holt, 1987. A poem for each day in a city boy's life.

Dunning, Stephen, Edward Lueders, and Hugh

Smith. *Reflections on a Gift of Watermelon Pickle.* Lothrop, 1988. Excellent anthology for students fourth grade and up.

Fleischman, Paul. *Joyful Noise: Poems for Two Voices.* HarperCollins, 1988. Poems about insects to be read aloud by two readers. Newbery Winner. Also *Big Talk: Poems for Four Voices.* Candlewick, 2000.

Fletcher, Ralph. *I Am Wings: Poems About Love.* Atheneum, 1994. Love poems for teens divided into "Falling In" and "Falling Out." Here are several other books you might enjoy: *Buried Alive: The Elements of Love.* Atheneum, 1996. *Ordinary Things: Poems from a Walk in Early Spring.* Atheneum, 1997. Encourages students to take a "metaphor walk" and find ideas in simple things. *Relatively Speaking: Poems About Family.* Orchard, 1997. Funny and serious poems told from the perspective of the younger of two brothers. *Have You Been to the Beach Lately?* Orchard, 2000. Poems from the point of view of a sixth-grade boy whose family comes to the beach and stays later than anyone else. *Water Planet: Poems about Water.* Arrowhead Books, 1990.

Fletcher, Tom. *Falling Through the Earth.* Mac An Leister Press, 1992.

George, Kristine O'Connell. *Old Elm Speaks: Tree Poems* (Clarion, 1998) and *The Great Frog Race and Other Poems* (Clarion, 1997). Wonderful! Also *Little Dog Poems* (Clarion, 1999) and *Toasting Marshmallows: Camping Poems* (Clarion, 2001).

Glaser, Isabel. *Dreams of Glory: Poems Starring Girls.* Atheneum, 1995. Celebrates the hopes, pride, fears, and determination of girls.

Graves, Donald. *Baseball, Snakes, and Summer Squash: Poems about Growing Up.* Boyd Mills, 1996. Gets at the nitty-gritty of what it's like to grow up as a boy.

Greenfield, Eloise. *Honey, I Love.* HarperCollins, 1986. Celebrates the daily life of a girl. Put a star next to this one.

Grimes, Nikki. *Something on My Mind.* Dial, 1986. Prose poems about a teenage girl's life.

Gunning, Monica. *Not a Copper Penny in My*

House: Poems from the Caribbean. Boyd Mills,
1999. Outstanding poetry, with stunning
illustrations.

Harley, Avis. *Fly with Poetry: An ABC of Poetry.*
Boyd Mills, 2000. Sensational book to
introduce kids to various poetic forms.

Ho, Minfong (trans.). *Maples in the Mist.*
Lothrop, Lee & Shepard, 1996. These are
classical poems, some 2,000 years old.
Gorgeous illustrations.

Hopkins, Lee Bennett. *Been to Yesterdays.* Boyd
Mills, 1995. Poignant and often painful
poems of this author's childhood.

Hopkins, Lee Bennett (ed.). *Best Friends.*
HarperCollins, 1984. Friendship poems,
with several gems. Also *Hand in Hand: An
American History Through Poetry.* Simon &
Schuster, 1994.

Janeczko, Paul. *That Sweet Diamond.* Atheneum,
1998. These baseball poems were penned
by a rabid fan and poet. Paul Janeczko
puts together the finest poetry antholo-
gies around, including *The Place My Words
Are Looking For* (Bradbury, 1990), *Poetry*

from A to Z (Bradbury, 1994), and *Pocket Poems* (Bradbury, 1985).

Johnson, Angela. *The Other Side: Shorter Poems.* Orchard, 2000. A young woman recounts thoughts about growing up in Shorter, Alabama. Potent!

Johnston, Tony. *It's about Dogs.* Harcourt, 2000. You'll love these dog poems!

Larrick, Nancy (ed.). *Piping Down the Valleys Wild.* Dell Yearling, 1999. An inexpensive anthology with both rhyming and non-rhyming poems.

Lewis, J. Patrick. *The Bookworm's Feast.* Penguin Putnam/Dial, 1999. Also *Freedom Like Sunlight: Praisesongs for Black Americans.* Creative Editions, 2000.

Livingston, Myra Cohn. *There Was a Place and Other Poems.* McElderry, 1988. Powerful poems about kids coping with difficult home situations.

Lyne, Sanford (ed.). *Ten-Second Rainshowers.* Simon & Schuster, 1996. A collection of terrific poems written by children of all ages. This book will spark lots of ideas for poems you can write!

Margolis, Richard. *Secrets of a Small Brother.* Simon & Schuster, 1991. Celebrates the good and bad moments between two brothers. Terrific.

Moore, Lilian. *I Feel the Same Way.* Atheneum, 1967. Subtle poems about feelings we share. Unusual rhyme schemes.

Morrison, Lillian. *At the Crack of the Bat.* Hyperion, 1992. Wonderful collection of baseball poems. Also *Slam Dunk.* Hyperion Books, 1995. Basketball poems.

Myers, Walter Dean. *Brown Angels.* HarperCollins, 1996. Moving poems sparked by turn-of-the-century photographs of African-American children.

Nye, Naomi Shihab (ed.). *What Have You Lost?* Greenwillow, 2001. A stirring collection of poems exploring loss, written by various poets for high-school kids.

Nye, Naomi Shihab, and Paul Janeczko (eds.). *I Feel a Little Jumpy Around You.* Simon & Schuster, 1996. The poems in this book are grouped in pairs to demonstrate the different ways in which male and female poets see the same topics.

Rosen, Michael (ed.). *Walking on the Bridge of Your Nose: Wordplay, Poems, and Rhymes.* Kingfisher, 1995.

Rylant, Cynthia. *The Soda Jerk.* Orchard, 1990. Poems from an adolescent boy working in an old-fashioned soda shop. Also *Waiting to Waltz: A Childhood.* Atheneum, 2001. Fine poems from the author's childhood.

Schertle, Alice. *Advice for a Frog* (Lothrop, 1995) and *Keepers* (Lothrop, 1992). Schertle is a marvelously clever poet. You must read her!

Sierra, Judy. *Antarctic Antics: A Book of Penguin Poems.* Harcourt, 1998. Funny, clever, imaginative poems that also teach content about penguins.

Soto, Gary. *A Fire in My Hands.* Scholastic, 1999. There is a poem in this book, "Oranges," that will knock your socks off. Also *Neighborhood Ode.* Econo-Clad Books, 1999.

Thomas, Joyce Carol. *Brown Honey in Broomwheat Tea.* HarperCollins, 1996. These poems are strong and stirring.

Turner, Ann. *Street Talk*. Houghton Mifflin, 1992. Poems that catch the drama of city life. For upper grades.

Wong, Janet S. *A Suitcase of Seaweed and Other Poems*. McElderry, 1996. This terrific collection explores the author's past, especially tensions between her Asian heritage and the American way of life. Also *Behind the Wheel: Poems about Driving* (McElderry/Simon & Schuster, 1999), and *Night Garden: Poems from the World of Dreams* (McElderry/Simon & Schuster, 2000).

Worth, Valerie. *All The Small Poems*. Farrar, Straus, 1996. Nobody writes better than Worth about the most ordinary things. In this book "earthworms glisten as fresh as new rubies dug out of deepest earth. . . ."